North East Life
in the 1960s

by Andrew Clark & Sharyn Taylor

An advert for Smiths furniture store from 1960 with special offers on bedroom suites, dining suites, settees and easy chairs. Also advertised is a '5-piece television suite to seat 7 persons – 3 seater settee, 3 chairs and one stool'. The price for the suite was $28^1/_2$ guineas. Their 'Magnificent Bedroom Suite' was priced at £65 19 shillings and 6d and included two double-door wardrobes and a dressing table with an Italian styled mirror. The bedroom suite was available on a payment plan of a 2 shilling deposit with 104 weekly payments of 12 shillings 6d. In 1960 Smiths had over 20 branches in the North East selling the popular furniture styles of the decade.

Copyright Andrew Clark & Sharyn Taylor 2018

First published in 2018 by

Summerhill Books
PO Box 1210
Newcastle-upon-Tyne NE99 4AH

www.summerhillbooks.co.uk

email: summerhillbooks@yahoo.co.uk

ISBN: 978-1-911385-22-6

Contents

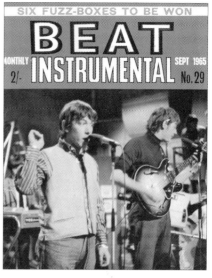

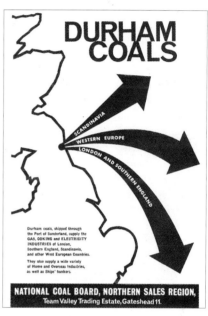

On 7th September 1968 a Durham Coast Rail Tour was organised. The locomotive 4472 Flying Scotsman conveyed railway enthusiasts from Huddersfield to Tyne Dock, South Shields. The passengers left the train, walked across the tracks and climbed into open wagons (*seen above*) with seats fitted specially for the occasion, then National Coal Board locomotives took them to Whitburn Colliery and around the South Shields area. This was a time when coal, transported by rail, was a vital fuel for use in the home and by industry.

Acknowledgements

The authors would like to thank the following who have kindly helped with this book:

Geoffrey Berriman, Alan Brett, John Carlson, Joyce Carlson, Harry & Pauline Clark, Ron Collins, Ron Curran, Philip Curtis, Anne Dixon, Valerie Dunmore, Tom Finch, Peter Gibson, Jack Hair, George Hoare, Tracy Johnson, Christopher Knapp, George Nairn, Francis Newman, Jim Pace, Bill Saunders, Mary Taylor and Leslie Took

The Chronicle, The Journal, Northern Echo, Sunderland Echo
Gateshead Library, Newcastle Library, North Tyneside Libraries
West Newcastle Picture History Collection, Alamy

Bibliography

A Hard Day's Write by Steve Turner, Carlton Books
Ashington Coal Company – The Five Collieries by Mike Kirkup, The People's History
Back of the Shaft – Memories of Murton by P.J. McPartland, Summerhill Books
Backworth Remembered by Bob Mitchelson, Summerhill Books
Gateshead Remembered by Anthea Lang, Summerhill Books
Houghton-le-Spring by Geoffrey Berriman, The People's History
Memories of Bedlingtonshire by Evan Martin, The People's History
Morpeth by Evan Martin & George Nairn, The People's History
South Shields by John Carlson & Joyce Carlson, The People's History
Southwick by Peter Gibson, The People's History
Wearside in Winter by Philip Curtis, Black Cat Publications

The interview with Sir Bobby Charlton was by Andrew Clark for Wear FM in 1992.
Raymond Soulsby's story is from *Around Stanley* by Alan Harrison & Jack Hair.
Shirley Grice's story is from *Wallsend Best* by Ron Curran.

Introduction

This book completes a series by the authors that remembers life in the North East from the 1930s up to the 1980s. In this volume we recall the memorable decade of the 1960s – thought by many to be one of the most exciting periods in our history.

We are thankful for the many people who have shared their stories of 1960s fashion, music, work, schooldays, music, entertainment, holidays and jazz bands.

Who can forget their first job at fifteen, straight from school and the excitement of your first pay packet – although most of the money probably went to your mam! Holidays were spent at the local seaside resorts such as Tynemouth, Whitley Bay or Seaburn and if you were lucky a week at Butlins in Filey.

The music scene had everything from Beatlemania, to local lads in The Animals achieving worldwide success and some of the great artists coming to the North East. The nightscene was vibrant with clubs such as the La Strada, in South Shields and Sunderland, and the La Dolce Vita in Newcastle where Tom Jones, at the height of his fame, appeared in 1966. Also in that year there was the greatest day in English football when England won the World Cup at Wembley and had in the team Bobby and Jackie Charlton from Ashington.

James Bolam and Rodney Bewes, stars of North East comedy series *The Likely Lads,* on the cover of the *Radio Times* (see page 28).

If any readers would like to share their memories (or spot themselves in photographs) we would be happy to hear from you. Please email us at: summerhillbooks@yahoo.co.uk

Andrew Clark & Sharyn Taylor

The Rising Sun Colliery Legionnaires Juvenile Jazz Band from Wallsend in 1966. From the late 1950s to the mid '70s jazz bands were very popular with young people. Bands representing their local communities would take part in competitions throughout the country. Led by their band master, the youngsters would be dressed in brightly coloured outfits with some holding a banner while others played their kazoos and various other musical instruments. For galas and other events the bands often paraded in formation through local streets (see page 11).

Snapshots of the 1960s

A Fab Decade

I loved the 1960s as it was such an exciting decade. I was born in 1948 so the '60s were my teenage years. In 1961 I was thirteen and for the next six years I enjoyed how vibrant everything seemed in my teens. I loved the fashions, the music and the nightlife. My favourite clothes were the long, flowing dresses that were popular during the hippy era. I liked my hair in a bouffant, platinum blond style as in the photograph of me on the right. Thinking back there were some brilliant groups and singers that I remember but the one I still like today has to be Tom Jones. When I turned eighteen I started going to nightclubs and a popular place where I lived in South Shields was the New Cellar Club. As the decade came to an end I was celebrating my twenty-first birthday. It was the end of a wonderful era.

Mary Taylor

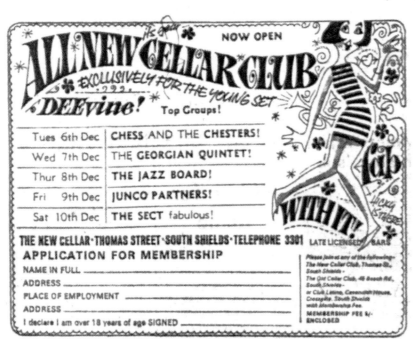

Left: An advert for the New Cellar Club in South Shields with the groups appearing in December 1966. The club was aimed 'exclusively for the young set' and in its advert uses some of the popular words and phrases of the time such as 'fab', 'with it' and 'deevine!' To apply for membership you had to declare you were over 18 years of age and also give your place of employment. One of the groups who were playing at the New Cellar Club in 1966 was The Jazz Board who had Nigel Olsson in their line up. Olsson later joined Elton John's backing band and continues to tour with him.

Right: Two young lads from Hetton-le-Hole, who are sporting the 'Rocker' look, get some help fixing their motorbike in 1960. Greased-back hair, leather jackets and motorbikes was the fashion for the Rockers in the 1960s. Their rivals were the Mods. Those lads had neater hair and wore Fred Perry polo shirts and parka coats while their mode of transport was a scooter. This era was the subject of the film *Quadrophenia*, directed by Stockton-born Franc Roddam in 1979, and based on an album by The Who.

Left: The number one hit *Summer Holiday* by Cliff Richard and The Shadows that was bought from Jeavons record store. The single was released in June 1963 and was the title track of the popular film. The Shadows also had a number one hit with the instrumental *Foot Tapper* which was also featured in the film. The band included two guitarists from the North East – Hank Marvin and Bruce Welch (who co-wrote *Summer Holiday*). In the early 1960s Jeavons had two shops in Newcastle (Percy Street and Pudding Chare) as well as ones on Wallsend High Street and in Skinnergate, Darlington. In recent years there has been a revival in the sale of vinyl records and in 2017 there were over four million LPs sold in the UK, the highest number since the early 1990s.

Right: The Beatles fooling around with the police at the height of their fame in the 1960s. When Beatlemania came to Newcastle in October 1963 the police were needed to control the crowds who queued for two days for tickets to a concert at the City Hall. When the box office opened there was a stampede and twenty-four people were hurt in the rush. Such was the demand to see The Beatles, the police issued a warning that only ticket-holders would be allowed near the City Hall the night of the performance on 23rd November 1963.

Three years later, The Beatles were causing a stir in Gateshead when they were banned from the junior record library which was launched in the town. Only short classical pieces were available and there was no pop section. Mrs Mary Bell, chairman of Gateshead's library committee, said: 'Pop music has got a hold on young people and tends to distract them from their homework. Even young children are copying The Beatles. I think children should have another form of music. Classical music is inspiring and I am sure it will educate them.'

Left: An advert for Ryle's of Whitley Bay from February 1967. They were launching the opening of their 'up to the minute department specially geared for the under 21s.'

Ryle's held fashion shows to showcase their spring and autumn collections and below, beside the company's van, is one of their models from spring 1967. She is wearing a grey wool dress, trimmed with red, and a red belt and buckle.

Left: An advert for the Austin cars on sale at the Osborne Garage, Newcastle in May 1969. The Maxi was priced at £978 16 shillings and 11d; the Austin 1300 was £766 10d while the Mini started at £622 8 shillings and 7d for a Mark 2 de lux (848 cc engine) up to £844 7 shillings 6d for the 1300 Countryman.

The Mini was launched in 1959 by the British Motor Corporation and designed by Sir Alec Issigonis. Over one million Mark I cars were sold and it became one of the classic designs of the 1960s. The performance model, the Mini Cooper, won the Monte Carlo Rally in 1964, '65 and '67. The Mark II model was launched in 1967 at the British Motor Show. Famously, three Mini Coopers were used as getaway cars for the robbery in the 1969 Michael Caine film *The Italian Job*.

The Mini is still in production almost sixty years after it was first launched and is now manufactured by the German car maker BMW. The cost of a basic model today is around £15,000.

Left: The Buist's petrol station on Etherstone Avenue, Newcastle in 1963. Before the days of self-service the assistant has come out of his booth to put petrol in the customer's car and take the money. The price of a gallon of petrol in 1963 was around five shillings. Fuel was sold in gallons up until the mid 1980s when the change over to litres was started by the suppliers. All petrol was sold in litres by the end of 1994.

Charles G.S. Buist Ltd sold Morris and MG cars from their showroom in Prudhoe Street, Newcastle and had branches in Darlington and Middlesbrough.

Right: The number 18 Newcastle Corporation bus on its way to the Leam Lane Estate, Gateshead via the Tyne Bridge. The yellow-liveried Leyland Titan bus is passing the Hancock Museum at Barras Bridge. Behind it is a white-sleeved policeman directing the traffic on this busy road. The wires of the trolleybus system, which was discontinued in October 1966, can be seen above the bus.

When We Were Young

Right: A group of youngsters from Elswick in Newcastle play in the street and fix their bikes in 1960. Their childhood was very different from today's young people. There was a lot more playing outside and electronic gadgets were only seen in science fiction films, TV and comics. These lads and lasses would be lucky if they had a television at home. Their games and playtime would be very much about imagination and some of their toys would be second-hand or home-made.

The days before wireless – a tin can telephone. We take mobiles or smart phones for granted today but in the 1960s very few homes had telephones. However, two tin cans and some string would provide hours of amusement.

Three fashionable young ladies enjoying a ride on the Waltzer at Houghton Feast around 1960. Rides such as these would have had the latest hit records of the day playing while you were spun around.

Marie Dixon demonstrates her hula-hoop in Leasingthorne, County Durham. The hula-hoop was launched in 1957 and, by the start of the 1960s, 100 million had been sold worldwide.

Another popular ride at Houghton Feast were the shuggy-boats, seen here in 1963.

Popular toys of the 1960s

1960 – Lego
Train sets
Etch-a-sketch

1961 – Airfix
Fuzzyfelt
Scalextric

1962 – Dinky toys
Corgi cars
Pogo sticks

1963 – Matchbox cars
Sindy doll
Diplomacy board game

1964 – Booma Boomerang
Mr Potato Head
Trolls

1965 – James Bond's Aston Martin
Dalek toys
Gonks

An advert for Dalek badges on sale at Woolworths.

1966 – Action Man
Tiny Tears
Thunderbirds toys

1967 – Spirograph
Johnny Astro space toys
Kerplunk

1968 – Beatles's Yellow Submarine
Joe 90 toys
Batman toys

1969 – Hot Wheels cars
Newton's Cradle
Space Hoppers

Some of the most popular toys of the 1960s were on sale at Parrish's in Shields Road, Newcastle – including: Action Man, Tiny Tears, Silver Cross Dolls' Prams and Meccano. Action Man, priced 32 shillings 11d, was advertised as: 'A completely new kind of soldier … Action Soldier, Sailor or Pilot. Over 11 inches tall, 21 moving parts, authentic weapons and equipment. Collect Action Man outfits – dozens to choose from.'

Plenty of toys were home-made – such as stilts, sledges, dolls houses, forts, garages and even soap box bogies like the ones above taking part in a race at Consett in 1960.

The Best Ten Years of My Life

The Rising Sun Legionnaires Juvenile Jazz Band was formed in 1964. This was a really big event in Wallsend, particularly with the pitmen and their families. The recruitment took place at the old Miners' Club on Station Road. We trained on Tuesday and Thursday nights from 6 to 7.30. The venue was then changed to the old Drill Hall on Vine Street, later to become the Community Centre. In the warmer weather and lighter nights we trained on the Rising Sun field which was brilliant, because nearly all of the competitions were out doors usually on fields. We loved it!

These were probably the best ten years of my life, as I retired at the ripe old age of 18. Some of my closest friends even to this day were involved in the band. It was our lives and nothing came between us and the band.

It taught us discipline and respect, and when John O'Shaunessy, who organised the band, said 'Jump' we just asked 'How High?' By the age of 14, I had moved through the ranks, from kazoo to being in the front row, and then my dream came true, I was made Band Major and Lynn O'Shaunessy was Drum Major. We felt so important, and everyone in the jazz band world knew us because we were the best. Happy Days!

Shirley Grice (formerly Shirley Sansom)

Shirley Sansom (centre) with Sandra and Rhoda Wilson.

Left: The Rising Sun Legionnaires in training on the colliery sports field in the mid 1960s.

Above and right: Three photographs of a jazz band parade through the village of Ryhope. Jazz bands were popular in the mining communities of Durham and Northumberland and in these images you can see the many people who have turned out to see the young people march past in their brightly coloured uniforms. The band members would spend many hours practising their marching, baton twirling and playing their instruments while mothers would form sewing groups to help make the uniforms.

Schooldays

Left: A woodwork class at St Thomas Aquinas Boys' School, Sunderland in 1964. The boys, in their clean white aprons, are making furniture.

The Boys' School had opened two years earlier at a cost of £165,638. St Thomas Aquinas Girls' School opened in April 1964 and cost £195,672. Three years later the school, like a number at that time, became a comprehensive with mixed classes.

The school was to last just twenty years and closed in 1986 due to falling numbers of pupils.

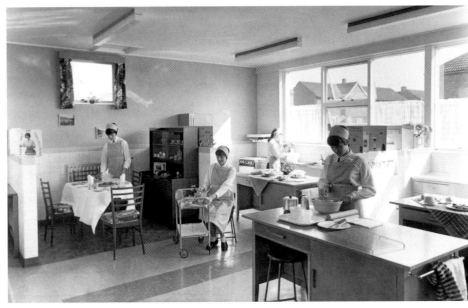

Left: A home economics class at St Thomas Aquinas Girls' School in 1964, the year it opened. The girl on the right is making cakes while another sets the table. Next to her, a pupil is arranging a tea set on a hostess trolley. A sign on the far left shows a housewife with the slogan: 'The Art of Entertaining'.

Getting the Cane and the Strap

At my school in Ashington you were caned in front of the whole school in assembly. If you played up in class, flicked paper around or such like, the teacher put a cross on a piece of paper next to your name. Too many crosses that week and you got the cane.

One day in assembly the headmaster said, 'Will Christopher Knapp come forward, please.' As he said it he was bending the cane over ready for me. 'I'm going to give you six of the best in front of everyone,' he said.

As I walked to the front someone shouted from the back of the hall, 'Give him six of the best, sir.' The headmaster just looked at the boy and said, 'You come forward and get the cane as well.'

The cane brought tears to your eyes and it made your backside sting so you made sure you didn't get it again. It hurt but it didn't hurt as much as everyone watching you get the punishment. It was embarrassing to get the cane in front of the whole school.

One time I got the strap and I tried to pull my hand away as the teacher went to hit me so he got two other pupils to hold my hand in place. I ended up with two marks on my hand. When I got home, my parents could see that I had been misbehaving. They also told me off and I was sent to my room.

Christopher Knapp

Left: Lollipop man George Lodge with primary school children from Lumley, near Chester-le-Street in 1967.

During the 1960s measures for greater safety were introduced on British roads due to ever increasing traffic. In 1967 the government brought in the Road Safety Act and one of its measures was to see lollipop men and women becoming more common around North East schools to help children cross busy roads.

A Teacher's Story

In the early 1960s I started my first year of teaching at a junior school in Bedlington under headmaster Henry Graham. Henry gave me a class of mixed ability 8-10 year olds. Like all primary school teachers, I covered every subject in the curriculum and tried to do it as taught at college. It took me some time to realise that good teaching performance has a lot to do with confidence and the relationship with the class which comes with experience.

My first visit from an inspector was late in the school year. It was a scorching hot July day. My charges were due to leave for secondary school and Miss White from County Hall, decided to visit at 2pm on the second last Friday of term. It was important for me to pass this inspection as I was in my probationary year on £42 a month and if I passed would increase my salary to £48 per month. Art was on the timetable and everybody was so shattered with the heat I had decided to give the class a free choice. When Miss White arrived Henry, my headmaster, came down and told me that a freedom of choice was out of the question. As the inspector was well into religious educational ideas, he suggested that she would appreciate a Biblical theme. We had been dealing with the Exodus with Moses leading the Hebrews out of Egypt for pastures new. 'Get them to crayon that,' announced Henry. 'She'll love it.'

Staff at Bedlington County Junior School, 1961. Evan Martin is front right. Headmaster Henry Graham is next to him.

The sugar paper was duly quartered, crayons handed out and off they went. Miss White appeared and was delighted that a Biblical theme was in motion and proceeded to move up the aisle to witness the various expressions of Moses and his tribe crossing the Red Sea. All was well until the desk of one of my pupils, Sheila Harper, was arrived at. Miss White gasped and enquired as to what Sheila was drawing. 'The Crossing of the Red Sea,' I confidently offered, although I was a good yard and a half away.

'No-one with the most vivid imagination could see this as part of the Exodus,' Miss White exclaimed. When I saw Sheila's effort, I could understand Miss White's disappointment. Moses was there, the Hebrews were there and the Red Sea was properly parted in the middle. Unfortunately for Sheila, me, and Miss White, Moses was driving a double decker United bus through the middle with the Hebrews hanging out the windows waving their goodbyes.

Sheila had been on the Sunday School trip to Crimdon Dene the previous weekend, in a bus, driven by the Chapel Minister. Its religious similarities with her religious instruction lessons at school produced the piece that afternoon. Miss White, who saw the funny side, said I was no longer a probationer and I could enjoy my summer holiday knowing I would be on £48 a month from September.

Evan Martin

The Big Freeze

Above and right: Ice on the River Tyne at Newcastle in early 1963, in the winter that became known as the 'Big Freeze'.

Christmas Day in 1962 was the coldest since the harsh winter of 1946/47. For the next ten weeks Britain was to suffer freezing conditions and heavy snow falls that brought chaos to the North East. On the 2nd January a blizzard began that went on for three days and the country was described as 'Iceberg Britain'. A week later gale force winds created giant snow drifts, in some places up to 15 feet high. People endured freezing nights and woke up to days where it snowed for several hours. Local councils had snow ploughs and gritters out every day to clear bus routes and main roads. Burst water pipes became a problem for many

households and warnings were given by the Water Companies of the dangers of lighting boilers when the pipes were frozen. The 22nd January was the coldest day of the winter and there was reports of anti-freeze in cars freezing up. On the first day of February snow fell for hours and this continued throughout the month. Schools were closed and travelling became more difficult. By the end of February local councils were cutting back on clearing roads because of the cost. Thankfully, the first week of March saw the beginning of a thaw and the Big Freeze was over.

Left: With snow drifts piled over ten feet high, a pathway needed to be cleared so the residents of this house could get to their front door.

These four photographs were taken near Burnopfield, County Durham in the winter of 1962/63.

Right: Snow piled high by the side of road near the Hobson Hotel.

Far right: A bus stop covered with snow shows how difficult it must have been for people to travel in these conditions.

The snow towers above Jim Scott.

A bulldozer is stuck in the snow at the Hobson Hotel.

The Big Flood

The extreme weather at the beginning of 1963 saw ice up to ten inches thick form on the River Wansbeck at Morpeth. When the thaw came on 7th March this caused the ice to melt and water flooded the town. Almost 500 homes were damaged as well as dozens of shops, businesses and factories. Cars struggled to drive along the streets of the Northumberland town (*right*). Morpeth had suffered a number of floods in the 19th century but the conditions seen in these photographs were rare for the 20th century.

Right: Two cyclists brave the water in Bridge Street, Morpeth in 1963.

In recent years there has been further flooding in the town – in 2008 and 2012 hundreds of properties were effected. It was estimated that the 2008 flood caused £20 million of damage.

Fashion

Above: A fashion show at Joplings department store in Sunderland in the late 1960s. The models are dressed in the latest styles of that time, however, two ladies in the audience are wearing the more traditional head scarf. The psychedelic stage design seen behind the models was by South Shields artist Tom Finch who was head of the Art Department at Joplings.

Right: An advert for the 'In-line fashion for today's teens' on sale at Joplings in October 1969. On the left is a 'trend-setting' tweed, Herringbone pattern coat in green and black. It was priced at £7 19 shillings 6d. On the right is a black, belted coat that was £16. This coat was an expensive luxury in 1969 when the average weekly wage was around £20.

The Mini Skirt

The fashion designer Mary Quant (*right*) is credited as popularising the mini skirt. She is said to have named it after her favourite car and another icon of the 1960s – the Mini Cooper.

Enid, a dress shop on the Great North Road in Newcastle, had this advertising slogan in 1968:

The long, the short or the tall.
The mini or maxi to enthral.
For day or for night we give you delight
with a size and a price for you all.

in LINE

JOPLINGS, SUNDERLAND

Above: Trend-setting Tweed. Herringbone pattern Coat with lots of fashion detail. Green/black. Teen fittings £7.19.6

Right: Black Beauty. Belted Coat featuring large revers. In-line fashion for today's teens £16

ON THE SECOND FLOOR

Joplings SUNDERLAND

MILAN HAJEK

BESPOKE TAILOR

CONTINENTAL AND ENGLISH STYLES

The best Footballers get their best suits from
MILAN HAJEK

Official Tailor for Newcastle United

An advert for Milan Hajek from 1963 – the official tailor of Newcastle United. In the 1960s the most stylish footballer of them all was George Best (*below*) who even opened his own boutique with Mike Summerbee of Manchester City.

YOUR NEW
CRIMPLENE
TROUSERS

FROM WALTONS

CRIMPLENE
FOR MEN

TAKES SOME BEATING

Literally. Wear them. Wash them. Stay out all night in them. Your new Crimplene uncrushables take it all in style. Won't crease—but stay creased in the right places. Get a crush on a pair of these superb lightweight trousers very soon. They won't mind in the least.

from £7.10.0.

Waltons
the home of good clothes

Right: In 1969 Isaac Waltons of Newcastle had Crimplene trousers on sale: 'Literally. Wear them. Wash them. Stay all night in them. Your new Crimplene uncrushables take it all in style. Won't crease – but stay creased in the right places. From £7 10 shillings.'

Fashions of the 1960s

Below are some of the popular fashions and styles of the decade:

Women's clothes

Capri trousers, mini skirts, hot pants, go go boots, sleeveless shift dresses, leather cat suits, flared trousers, bell bottoms, psychedelic prints, leather coats, velvet dresses, kaftans and ponchos.

Hair styles

Bee hive, back combing, long straight hair, chin length contour and page boy.

Fashion Icons

Brigitte Bardot, Jackie Kennedy, Cathy McGowan, Jean Shrimpton and Twiggy.

Cathy McGowan, presenter of *Ready Steady Go!* on the cover of the *TV Times* in 1965.

Men's clothes

Tailored suits with skinny ties, Levi jeans, Beatles suits, mariner's hats, polo shirts, parkas, Gannex raincoats, crimplene trousers, sandals, frock coats, ruffle shirts and kipper ties.

Hair styles

Flat top, greaser, mop tops, moustaches, beards, side burns and long hair.

Fashion Icons

George Best, The Beatles, Michael Caine, and Mick Jagger.

Working Life

My First Job

In 1961, when I was fifteen, I worked for Smith's furnishing company in the office at King Street, South Shields. It was a poorly paid job but I have lovely memories of it. We were like family. I was office junior and some older girls were book-keepers. There were typewriters tapping away all day. My job was to file people's documents and arrears and go to the post office for stamps. A lady cleaner called Cathy used to sing all day and make the tea. We had good tea breaks and an hour and half for lunch. When a woman got married it was automatic she left her job. That was common then and quite a lot of women came and went. If a widow with children applied, she would be taken on as she had responsibilities. Near five o'clock our boss would look at his watch and we all stood up to attention and waited for the signal from him. Then right on five he would nod his head and all the girls would clash down the shutters of the book-keeping cabinets. It was time to go home.

Valerie Dunmore

Valerie Dunmore (née Clemens), aged 15, outside her house in Hylton Avenue, South Shields, during her first week at work.

First Wage

I left school in July 1965, one month after my fifteenth birthday. Within a few weeks I started my first job at Brian Mills in Sunderland where I helped to process catalogue orders. Everyone in my class got a job and many were arranged by the school. That's what it was like in the 1960s. My first wage was about £4 10 shillings and I gave half of this money to my mam.

I then got a new job at Plessey's electronic factory on North Hylton Road in Sunderland. It was so easy to move from one job to another back then. The wages were better than Brian Mills and I was earning over £5 a week.

Pauline Clark

Christine Elizabeth Honnor, from Murton, County Durham was featured in an advert for Dewhirst's clothing factory in Peterlee in 1969. Christine said: 'I love it here … working at Dewhirst's.' The firm was offering new recruits: 'Better Pay. Better Conditions. Understanding Care.'

Workers assembling electronic products at Plessey's factory in Sunderland.

Right: The *Barbara* at Laing's fitting-out quay on the Wear in 1962. The ship was built for a Swedish owner with the custom in that country to keep the name of the vessel a secret until it is launched. When the *Barbara* was launched from Laing's on 4th May 1962, the name was covered up and as the ship went down the slipway a yellow drape was

removed to reveal her name. In the background is Wearmouth Colliery which was closed and demolished in the 1990s and is now the site of Sunderland's Stadium of Light.

Working in the Shipyards

When I started work in the shipyards my first wage in September 1966 was £3 2s 7d (£3.13) to take home. Out of that was £2 board to my mother which left £1 2s 7d pocket money. One of my friends had a job in a cafe and others worked as labourers and their take home pay was twice as much as mine. But that, I suppose, was the sacrifice we apprentices had to make before we came into the 'big money' when we came out of our time. The big money carrot was more like a big joke as apprentices at that time continued to be used as a cheap source of labour.

For the cold conditions in the yard my dad gave me a coat which a mate at work had given him. It sticks in my memory because of its comparison to the radical 1960s fashions of the time. The large dress coat was grey with prominent chalk stripes, double breasted and padded shoulders. It was like something from a gangster movie. Florrie, my mother-in-law, had knitted me a woollen hat, and I was surprised how much heat a scarf could keep in. I bought a pair of steel toe-capped boots from the shipyard store. Five shillings were docked from my wages until they were paid for which put a big hole in my weekly take home pay.

Peter Gibson

The huge supertanker *Esso Northumbria* (*left*) was built at Swan Hunter's in Wallsend and launched on 2nd May 1969 by Princess Anne. Ships such as *Esso Northumbria* were built at a time when the Suez Canal was blocked by Egypt following their war with Israel in 1967. With tankers now having to sail the long journey from the Persian Gulf around the Cape of Good Hope these massive vessels were designed to carry as much crude oil as possible to the refineries in Europe.

Right: One of the last coal trains to leave Ryhope Colliery, County Durham in October 1966. The following month the pit was closed.

The train was heading for Sunderland which, as can be seen in the early 1960s advert below, was the starting point for coal exports to Scandinavia and Western Europe as well as to London and Southern England.

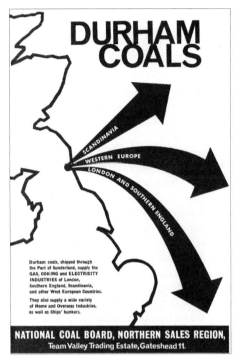

The demolition of the pithead at Ryhope in 1969.

Another North East pit that was closed in the 1960s was the Rising Sun Colliery in Wallsend.

Right: The four men who were in the last cage when the Rising Sun Colliery ceased production in 1969.

As the pits were closing in Northumberland and Durham, miners were encouraged to move to collieries that had a longer working life. On the right is an advert from 1969 for jobs that were available at Cotgrave in Nottinghamshire and Kellingley in North Yorkshire. The men were being offered: 'Six paid statutory holidays, two weeks paid annual leave and seven additional rest days per annum with pay.'

Sounds of the 1960s

One of the most successful British groups of the early 1960s was The Shadows. Originally known as Cliff Richard's backing band they went on to have many hits themselves. Two of the band were Hank Marvin and Bruce Welch from the North East.

Marvin was born Brian Robson Rankin in Newcastle in 1941 and in his early days played the banjo and piano. He changed to the guitar after listening to Buddy Holly. His stage name comes from a childhood nickname of Hank and the singer Marvin Rainwater. Bruce Welch grew up in Chester-le-Street and in the 1950s formed a skiffle group with Marvin who he met while attending Rutherford Grammar School in Newcastle. In 1958 they travelled to London to take part in a talent competition and stayed in the capital to pursue a musical career. In the same year they were asked to join Cliff Richard's band, The Drifters, who later changed to The Shadows after a dispute with an American group with the same name.

With Cliff Richard they had number one singles in 1959 with *Living Doll* and *Travellin' Light*. The following year they had their first number one without Richard's vocals with *Apache* (*re-released on the EP The Shadows To The Fore, shown right*). Further instrumental hit singles followed with *Kon-Tiki*, *Wonderful Land*, *Dance On* and *Foot Tapper*. With Cliff Richard they also recorded *The Young Ones*, *Bachelor Boy* and *Summer Holiday* that all topped the charts. The Shadows continued to record and tour up until 1968 when they broke up and Hank Marvin went on to have a successful solo career. The Shadows reformed several times and in 2009 they went on a 50th anniversary tour.

The Animals (*left*) were formed in Newcastle in 1962 and the original line-up was Eric Burdon (vocals), Alan Price (keyboards), Hilton Valentine (guitar), Bryan 'Chas' Chandler (bass) and John Steel (drums). Their first single was *Baby Let Me Take You Home* in 1964 which reached number 21 in the charts. The follow up, *The House of The Rising Sun*, was to make them worldwide stars. Their arrangement of this traditional folk song, with Burdon's howling vocals, Valentine's guitar riffs and Price's organ playing, was number one in the UK and America. Eric Burdon had first heard the song when it was performed by North East folk singer Johnny Handle in a club in Newcastle.

The Animals followed up *The House of The Rising Sun* with further hits: *Don't Let Me Be Misunderstood*, *We Gotta Get Out Of This Place*, *It's My Life* and *Don't Bring Me Down*. The group toured America and performed on television on *The Ed Sullivan Show*. The Animals also appeared in a Hollywood movie, *Get Yourself a College Girl*, with the London group The Dave Clark Five. This was the time of the so called 'British Invasion' when UK bands dominated the music scene in America.

In 1965 Alan Price left The Animals to concentrate on his own career. The following year the first incarnation of the group was disbanded to be replaced by Eric Burdon and The Animals. In later years the original members got back together for tours and recording before breaking up for the final time in 1984.

Right: Eric Burdon and Chas Chandler on the cover of the magazine *Beat Instrumental* from September 1965.

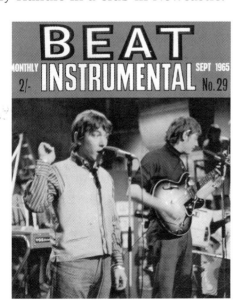

John Lennon and Paul McCartney wrote the song *She Loves You* in Newcastle after playing at the Majestic Ballroom on 26th June 1963. The song was written in a hotel room believed to be in

the Royal Turks Head in Grey Street (*below*). There were plans to place a plaque on the building to commemorate the song, however, Paul McCartney could not remember if they had stayed at the hotel or one in Jesmond and plans for the plaque were dropped.

Tom Jones appeared at the La Dolce Vita nightclub, Newcastle in December 1966 – the year of his big hit *Green, Green Grass of Home*. Seats to see the singer were bookable

for five shillings per person but there was a limited number available. Fifty years later, Tom Jones is as popular as ever and has a new generation of fans from his appearances on the TV talent show *The Voice*.

The most popular album of 1967 was *Sgt. Pepper's Lonely Hearts Club Band* by The Beatles. The album's cover is a collage of over 50 famous people including Wallsend-born footballer Albert Stubbins (*left*) who played for Newcastle and Liverpool.

The most popular singles of the 1960s

1960 – It's Now or Never
by Elvis Presley

1961 – Wooden Heart
by Elvis Presley

1962 – I Remember You
by Frank Ifield

1963 – She Loves You
by The Beatles

1964 – Can't Buy Me Love
by The Beatles

1965 – Tears
by Ken Dodd

1966 – Green, Green Grass of Home
by Tom Jones

1967 – Release Me
by Engelbert Humperdinck

1968 – Hey Jude
by The Beatles

1969 – Sugar, Sugar
by The Archies

The most popular albums

1960 – South Pacific
Soundtrack to the film

1961 – G.I. Blues
by Elvis Presley

1962 – West Side Story
Soundtrack to the film

1963 – With The Beatles
by The Beatles

1964 – Beatles for Sale
by The Beatles

1965 – The Sound of Music
Soundtrack to the film

1966 – The Sound of Music

1967 – Sgt. Pepper's Lonely Hearts
Club Band
by The Beatles

1968 – The Sound of Music

1969 – Abbey Road
by The Beatles

While on tour with The Animals, Chas Chandler saw a guitarist playing in a club in Greenwich Village, New York in 1966. That guitarist was Jimi Hendrix (*right*) and Chandler, spotting a rare talent, persuaded him to come to Britain with him. For a time Hendrix stayed at Chandler's house in Newcastle and he also produced the American's first single *Hey Joe* that reached the top ten in January 1967. In February of that year the Jimi Hendrix Experience played at the New Cellar Club in South Shields and the following month at Club A'Gogo in Newcastle. Chas Chander also produced the singles *Purple Haze* and *Foxy Lady* and the albums *Are You*

Experienced and *Axis: Bold as Love*. It was during the recording of Hendrix's third and final album, *Electric Ladyland*, that a dispute with Chandler led to a parting of the ways. In 1969 Jimi Hendrix was the headline act at the American music festival Woodstock. Sadly, the following year he died in London following a drug overdose.

Chas Chandler continued to discover new talent in the 1970s when he managed and produced the band Slade who had six number one hits in the UK. In the 1990s he was the driving force behind the building of the Newcastle Arena.

In September 1968 the musical *Hair* was first performed in London. The controversial show featured songs such as *The Age of Aquarius* which celebrated hippy counter culture. The original West End cast included Paul Nicholas, Elaine Paige, Oliver Tobias and South Shields-born J. Vincent Edwards (*left in a publicity photograph by the Thames*).

In the 1960s Edwards sang in local bands The Invictors and The Answers before turning to song writing. He co-wrote *Right Back Where We Started From* which was a number two hit for Maxine Nightingale in 1976.

Right: Alan Price and Bob Dylan during the filming of the documentary *Dont Look Back*. Directed by D.A. Pennebaker, the film followed Dylan as he toured Britain in 1965 and includes his time in Newcastle when he appeared at the City Hall. The American singer is filmed clothes shopping at Marcus Price in the Groat Market, Newcastle and spending time with Alan Price. During a discussion about the folk singer Donovan, Price says he is 'a good bloke' and Dylan repeats the words, putting on a North East accent.

The documentary memorably starts with Dylan holding and discarding cards with words from the song *Subterranean Homesick Blues*.

Bob Dylan returned to Newcastle in 1984 to perform in front of a packed crowd at St James' Park.

Folk Memories

I saw Bob Dylan play at the Odeon in Newcastle in 1966. The first half of the concert was an acoustic set and for the second half he changed to electric with a backing band. The year before, Dylan had been booed at the Newport Folk Festival when he used an electric guitar. This did not go down well with some of his fans who said it was against the folk roots of his music. I remember there was some heckling from the audience at the Odeon during the electric part of the concert but the change of style did not bother me.

I was a big folk fan in the 1960s and I would go to the George and Dragon in Sunderland to see local musicians play. They ran a folk club at the pub and the compere was Mike Elliott who later became well known as 'Mike the Mouth' on local radio. One of the best folk singers I saw at the George and Dragon was Ed Pickford. He wrote a song about the Seaham Harbour Lifeboat disaster when nine people were killed in 1962. A great song I remember Pickford singing was *The Day They Tried to Bomb the Torrey Canyon* about the oil tanker that was bombed by planes after it ran aground off the south coast.

Harry Clark

1960s Music Time Line

1960

April 16th – Eddie Cochran, Gene Vincent and Cochran's girlfriend Sharon Sheeley are injured in a car accident in Wiltshire. Cochran died in hospital the following day.

August 1st – The Beatles make their first appearance under that name in Germany. The line-up was John Lennon, Paul McCartney, George Harrison, Stuart Sutcliffe and Pete Best.

August 25th – The Shadows' instrumental *Apache* reaches number one in the UK charts.

1961

February 9th – The Beatles perform at the Cavern Club in Liverpool for the first time.

October 5th – *Kon-Tiki* by The Shadows goes to number one in the UK single charts.

December 13th – *The Young Ones* film, starring Cliff Richard and featuring The Shadows, has its premier in London.

1962

March 22nd – *Wonderful Land* by The Shadows goes to number one.

May 26th – *Stranger on the Shore* by Acker Bilk goes to number one in America and is the biggest selling single in the US that year. The instrumental was also a massive hit in Britain after it was used as the theme for a TV drama.

July 12th – The Rolling Stones play their first gig at the Marquee Club in London.

August 15th – Ringo Starr joins The Beatles and replaces Pete Best on drums.

August 17th – *Telstar* by The Tornados is released in the UK. The single was a hit around the world and The Tornados became the first UK group to top the American charts.

October 5th – The Beatles release their first single, *Love Me Do*.

An advert for Acker Bilk at the Latino club, South Shields in 1966. Also advertised are Peter & Gordon whose greatest hit was *A World Without Love* written by Lennon and McCartney.

1963

January 24th – *Dance On* by The Shadows tops the UK charts. The previous number one was *Bachelor Boy* with Cliff Richard and The Shadows.

March 22nd – The Beatles release their first album, *Please Please Me*.

June 7th– The Rolling Stones' first single *Come On* is released.

August 9th– The first episode of the music show *Ready Steady Go!* is broadcast by ITV.

September 12th – *She Loves You* becomes The Beatles first number one in the UK.

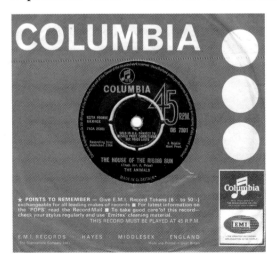

1964

January 1st – *Top of the Pops* is broadcast for the first time on the BBC.

June 26th – The Rolling Stones release *It's All Over Now* – their first number one in the UK.

July 9th – The Animals' *The House of The Rising Sun* (*left*) goes to number one in the UK.

August 4th – *You Really Got Me* is released by The Kinks.

September 5th – *The House of The Rising Sun* tops the American singles chart.

1965

January 23rd – *Downtown* by Petula Clark goes to number one in the USA.

May 5th – Alan Price leaves *The Animals*. He is replaced by Mick Gallagher and then Dave Rowberry.

October 29th – The Who release *My Generation*.

1966

April 21st – Alan Price reaches number nine in the charts with the single *I Put A Spell On You*.

August 5th – The Beatles release the album *Revolver* and the double-A side single *Eleanor Rigby / Yellow Submarine*.

December 16th – *Hey Joe* the first single by The Jimi Hendrix Experience is released.

1967

April 8th – Sandie Shaw with *Puppet on a String* wins the Eurovision Song Contest.

May 17th – *Dont Look Back*, a documentary film featuring Bob Dylan, is premiered.

June 1st – The Beatles release the album *Sgt. Pepper's Lonely Hearts Club Band*.

June 25th – The Beatles perform *All You Need Is Love* for the first time during *Our World*, a worldwide television special.

September 30th – The BBC launch Radio 1 with Tony Blackburn playing *Flowers in the Rain* by The Move.

November 8th – *San Franciscan Nights* by Eric Burdon and The Animals goes to number eight in the charts.

1968

April 6th – Cliff Richard with *Congratulations* finishes second in the Eurovision Song Contest at the Royal Albert Hall.

September 27th – The musical *Hair* opens in London.

December 22nd – The Animals reunite for a benefit concert at the Newcastle City Hall.

1969

January 12th – Led Zeppelin release their debut album.

January 30th – The Beatles perform for the last time in public on the roof of the Apple building in London.

March 29th – *Boom Bang-a-Bang* sung by Lulu is the joint winner of the Eurovision Song Contest.

July 5th – The Rolling Stones play a free concert in Hyde Park. During the concert Mick Jagger reads a eulogy for former guitarist Brian Jones who had died two days before.

August 15th to 18th – The Woodstock music festival takes place.

The cover of *I Put A Spell On You* by The Alan Price Set.

Hey Joe, the first single by The Jimi Hendrix Experience, produced by Chas Chandler.

The soundtrack of the musical *Hair* featuring J. Vincent Edwards from South Shields.

Happy Holidays

A group of youngsters sit on the sewerage pipe at Tynemouth in the summer of 1960. Other popular North East seaside destinations at that time were Whitley Bay, Cullercoats, South Shields, Newbiggin-by-the-Sea, Redcar, Roker and Seaburn.

Great Days at Seaburn

Seaburn was the place to go at weekends, Bank Holidays and the annual shipyard fortnight during the summer months. Families, friends and neighbours gathered in groups at their favourite spot to enjoy the simple pleasures of a day at the seaside. There are memories of queuing for hot water at Notarianni's to make tea on the beach; sandy sandwiches and chips – with fish if you could afford it; as well as donkey rides, making sandcastles and plodgin'. The activities were occasionally disturbed by an announcement over the public address system that a child had been found. The child's description was usually accompanied by distraught wailing in the background. For those looking for other things to do at Seaburn there was the boating pool, crazy golf, the miniature railway and, of course, the fair which was dominated by the impressive Big Dipper. In recent years, however, people have found other ways to spend their leisure time and the days when families had to arrive at the beach early in the morning to secure a decent place have long gone.

Peter Gibson

A postcard, sent from Sunderland to Darlington in August 1962, of the boating lake and amusement park at Seaburn. On the back of the postcard is the message: 'Having a lovely time, weather not too bad.'

Hi-de-Hi!

The practice of going by air to destinations abroad in quest of guaranteed sunshine took off in the 1960s. Before then, Butlins at Filey on the North Yorkshire coast was the favourite holiday destination for many. The holidays were affordable and were all inclusive.

Accommodation was in quaint but serviceable chalets, which were constructed in neat, colourful rows, separated by spacious lawns and ornamented by flower beds. Meals were taken at one of several dining halls, and all entertainment was free. Only drinks from the numerous on site bars had to be paid for. Filey was laid out roughly in the form of a grid, the focal point being the swimming and diving pool, the scene of many regattas, where swimmers were pitted in competition with one another for the amusement of their fellow campers.

The Redcoats were the cheerleaders and motivators for the campers. To be a Redcoat you had to be a good mixer. If you passed one, you could expect to be hailed with the Butlins catch-phrase, 'Hi-de-Hi!' a greeting said to have been borrowed from Cab Calloway, an American jazz singer. Or you could take the initiative in greeting them, and be acknowledged by the cheery rejoinder 'Ho-de-Ho!'

Redcoats stood out from the crowd in their bright red blazers and cream slacks, or pleated skirts in the case of the women, although both men and women sometimes wore shorts.

Throughout the day, when not supervising sporting contests, the Redcoats would be kept busy overseeing numerous events that took place indoors. If they weren't co-

Two postcard views of the Butlins holiday camp in Filey.

ordinating the fancy dress parade, they might be judging the entrants in such disparate categories as bonny babies or glamorous grandmothers.

The day began with a waking call from Radio Butlin, and a reminder that breakfast would be served in the dining hall shortly. Having your meals served by polite, dining room staff was a pleasurable experience, especially, I imagine, for normally hard pressed wives and mothers who, for fifty one weeks in the year, fulfilled that function themselves, after having first cooked the meals. The food was plain, nothing fancy, but wholesome and appetizing. The waiters and waitresses were invariably pleasant, even if they always seemed to be rushed off their feet. When one of them dropped a plate, the whole building erupted into cheers as it hit the floor. There was never a mealtime when it didn't happen, which led me to wonder if they didn't drop plates on purpose. Had they been instructed to sacrifice the odd plate to enliven the place and contribute to the *esprit de corps*, the sense of sharing in the fun of a Butlins holiday?

P.J. McPartland

TV Times

Right: The cast of *The One O'clock Show* which was broadcast on weekdays by Tyne Tees Television. Over 1,000 episodes of the variety show were produced in its five-year run starting in 1959. The cast included: Shildon-born singer George Romaine, Austin Steele, Terry O'Neill, Shirley Wilson, Chris Langford and Jack Haig as Wacky Jackie (front right, wearing the bowler hat). Jack Haig continued to appear on television for the next forty years and his final role was playing a member of the French resistance in *'Allo 'Allo*.

Tyne Tees Television was launched on 15th January 1959. Two of the guests on a special show on the channel's opening night were North East actors Bill Travers (see page 38) and his sister Linden. Linden Travers is best known for her role in the Alfred Hitchock film *The Lady Vanishes*.

Left: Rodney Bewes and James Bolam – *The Likely Lads*. The classic comedy set in the North East, written by Dick Clement and Monkseaton-born Ian La Frenais, was first shown on the BBC on 16th December 1964 and ran for 20 episodes. Unfortunately, many of these are now lost as the BBC had a policy of wiping tapes of recordings that they thought were of no interest. The series was brought back in 1973 as *Whatever Happened To The Likely Lads* (see *North East Life in the 1970s*).

Right: Wendy Craig, with Ronald Hines, in *Not in Front of the Children*. The actress, who was born in Sacriston, County Durham was first known for her dramatic roles in films such as *The Servant* and *The Nanny*. However, she found greater success playing housewives in comedies such as *Not in Front of the Children* (1967-70), ... *And Mother Makes Three* (1971-73), ... *And Mother Makes Five* (1974-76) and *Butterflies* (1978-83). As a child, Wendy attended Durham High School for Girls and she returned in 2007 to open a new building named in her honour.

Left: John Woodvine, who was born at Tyne Dock, South Shields, is a very familiar face on television. In the 1960s he appeared in *Danger Man*, *The Saint*, *Z Cars*, *Softy Softly* and *Emergency-Ward 10*. In 1969 he returned to his North East roots in *Close the Coalhouse Door*, which was broadcast by the BBC in their series *The Wednesday Play*. Originally written for the Newcastle Playhouse by Alan Plater, it was a history of the mining industry seen through the eyes of a Durham family and was based on stories by Shildon author Sid Chaplin. Songs were written by Gateshead musician Alex Glasgow.

In more recent years John Woodvine has been seen in the Tyneside productions *Hebburn* and *Vera* as well as *Coronation Street*, *Holby City*, *Emmerdale*, *Midsomer Murders* and *The Crown*.

Radio Times

SIXPENCE   LONDON AND SOUTH-EAST

BBC-1 tv BBC-2

DR. WHO
on the
Web Planet
SEE PAGE 3

Doctor Who, seen here on the cover of the *Radio Times*, was first shown on 23rd November 1963. William Hartnell was the Doctor and one of his assistants in the first two series, Ian Chesterton, was played by Sunderland-born actor William Russell (*seen above, third from the left*). Hartnell was replaced as the Doctor by Patrick Troughton in 1966. Fifty years (and a dozen Doctors) later, the show is still as popular as ever.

Colin Welland, James Ellis, Joseph Brady and Brian Blessed in a scene from the police drama *Z Cars*. Launched in 1962, over 800 episodes were produced and it made stars of actors such as Stratford Johns and Frank Windsor. North East writers Alan Plater and James Mitchell contributed scripts to the series and South Shields-born Ridley Scott made his directorial debut with an episode in 1965. Scott went on to a successful film career and directed, amongst others, *Alien*, *Blade Runner* and *Gladiator* (*see North East Life in the 1980s*).

Popular TV shows of the 1960s

Comedies

At Last the 1948 Show, Not Only … But Also, Steptoe and Son, The Likely Lads, The Rag Trade, Till Death Us Do Part and Up Pompeii!

Dramas

The Avengers, Danger Man, Dr Finlay's Casebook, The Champions, The Forsyte Saga, The Human Jungle, Maigret, The Power Game, The Prisoner, Softly, Softly, The Wednesday Play and Z-Cars.

DANGER MAN ANNUAL

Starring Patrick McGoohan as John Drake from the famous TELEVISION SERIES

Patrick McGoohan on the cover of the *Danger Man* annual. The spy series was first shown in 1960. Seven years later McGoohan produced *The Prisoner* where he played Number Six trapped in a mysterious village

American shows

The Addams Family, Batman, The Beverly Hillbillies, Bewitched, Bonanza, Lost in Space, Star Trek, The Man from Uncle, The Munsters and Voyage to the Bottom of the Sea.

Children's shows

Animal Magic, Captain Scarlet and the Mysterons, Doctor Who, The Flintstones, Joe 90, Look and Read, Space Patrol, Stingray, The Magic Roundabout and Thunderbirds.

Quizzes and other shows

Opportunity Knocks, Ready Steady Go, Pick of the Pops, Take Your Pick, That Was The Week That Was and What's My Line.

Bricks, Mortar and Concrete

In the mid 1960s some of the old colliery streets in the Northumberland village of Backworth were in a very poor state and without basic modern facilities. The demolition of these houses started in 1965 and here are Mr John Scott and his son-in-law who were the last to leave the pit cottages.

Right: An advert for the homes that Leech were building in the North East in 1965. The flat-roofed house shown was priced from £2,750 and included a garage and wash-house. In the 1960s and '70s, Leech built hundreds of houses like this in the new town of Cramlington. The builder and the local council offered easy payment terms to workers in the town's factories. With a £50 deposit the council would arrange a 100% mortgage to the buyer.

Also featured in this advert is a bungalow, including a garage, that was priced from £2,450.

By the mid 1960s Leech had built over 60,000 homes in the North East and they were offering: 'houses for every income group on more than twenty-five garden estates. Leech Houses are the easiest of all to purchase – low price – inclusive of legal charges – only a deposit to pay.'

At this time Leech were building estates in Newcastle, Gateshead, Sunderland, Washington, Durham, Chester-le-Street, Hebburn, Jarrow, Seaton Delaval and Stakeford.

Our First Home

My parents were married in 1967 and at first they 'lived in' with my grandparents. After a few months they got their first home which was an upstairs Tyneside flat. It was very run down but Dad was handy and he made it a nice cosy place for them. They had an outside toilet shared with their downstairs neighbours and a tap in the backyard. Both Mam and Dad had moved out of the lovely council houses of their parents who had got these homes after the Second World War and their living conditions were so much better than this flat. My grandparents' homes had inside toilets and bathrooms as well as a lovely garden. No such luxuries for my parents!

I came along in 1968 and it must have been difficult for Mam to look after a baby when all the water had to be brought up a flight of stairs from the yard. After a couple of years we got a council flat which, thankfully, had an indoor bathroom. In the 1970s my parents were able to afford to buy their first house. It only cost a few thousand pounds which seems so cheap when compared with today's prices.

Whenever I watch those old black and white films from the early '60s, such as *A Kind of Loving* and *Saturday Night and Sunday Morning,* I wonder if this is what my early life was like. Those films always seemed to be about struggling young couples with a baby.

Tracy Johnson

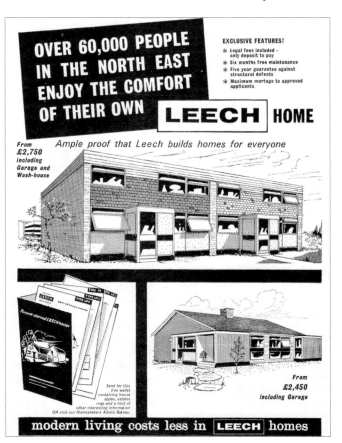

The 1960s saw great changes in housing in the North East. In Newcastle, dozens of streets made up of terraced houses and flats were demolished. At that time there was a trend for town planners to believe that it was best that these streets should be replaced by multi-storey flats. On the right, one of these tower blocks is being constructed in Walker.

Other tower blocks were built in the West End of Newcastle to replace the old streets that were pulled down around Scotswood Road.

Left: The Gateshead car park, opened in 1969, which became famous as one of the locations for the Michael Caine film *Get Carter* (*see North East Life in the 1970s*).

Built for £200,000, the multi-storey car park was an example of brutalism architecture which was popular and cutting edge at that time. However, the structure had a number of flaws. It was meant to open at Christmas 1968 but that was set back by ten months. The raw concrete suffered in the North East weather and within a few years patches appeared on its surface. The car park, with the adjoining shopping centre, was demolished in 2010 and fragments sold off in commemorative tins.

On 14th November 1968 King Olav V of Norway (*seen above taking off his hat*) opened Newcastle's Civic Centre (*above*). At the official ceremony the King said: 'I am sure this new and splendid building will be a proud token of Newcastle's growth and development. May it prove a blessing to this ancient city and its people.' The foundation stone for the Civic Centre was laid on 30th November 1960 and the first phase of the building was completed three years later at a cost of £2,500,000. Construction of the second phase, costing £2,355,000, was carried out between May 1965 and November 1968.

Football Highlights

One of the great teams of the 1960s was Manchester United with their forward line of Bobby Charlton (*right*), Denis Law and George Best. In 1964 Sunderland played United in the sixth round of the FA Cup and the memorable game is recalled here by Bobby Charlton:

'Manchester United and Sunderland drew 3-3 at Old Trafford – we had scored two goals in the last few minutes to get a replay at Roker Park. By the time we came up to Sunderland on the Wednesday it wasn't an all-ticket match, anyone could get in. They wouldn't have allowed it these days. There was so many people trying to get in the ground they knocked the big gates down and, although the official attendance was 45,000, I think there was more like 80,000 inside.

'At Roker Park we were again getting beat but I equalised with a header in the last minute of extra-time. It was so exciting. Then eventually we went to Huddersfield for the third match and we were behind at half time but eventually ran out 5-1 winners. The three matches were so exciting but took so much out of us that a few days later we played the semi-final against West Ham and got beat easily. Those were three memorable games against Sunderland and I think were one of best series of matches I've ever played in.'

Although Ashington-born Bobby left the North East as a teenager, he has great fondness for the fans in the region:

'In the first game at Old Trafford there was so many Sunderland people down and they were really going for it. They were in the Second Division then but they were doing quite well. Charlie Hurley was the captain. There was a phenomenal atmosphere at the games with really knowledgeable football people.'

Left: The programme for the FA Cup replay at Roker Park. Sunderland drew the first game at Old Trafford 3-3. The replay at Roker Park ended 2-2 with United winning the second replay at Huddersfield 5-1.

Although beaten in the FA Cup, Sunderland went on to win promotion to the First Division at the end of the season.

Right: Sunderland players take a break from training in the mid 1960s. Included are a number who were in the team against Manchester United: Martin Harvey, George Herd, Johnny Crossan, Nicky Sharkey, Len Ashurst and Jimmy Montgomery. Kneeling, third from the left, is Brian Clough who missed the whole of the 1963-64 season through injury.

In 1969 Newcastle United won the Inter-Cities Fairs Cup by beating Ujpesti Dozsa from Hungary in a two-legged final. In the previous round United were drawn against Glasgow Rangers in what would become an infamous night at St James' Park on 21st May 1969. The first game at Ibrox had ended goalless and for the return an army of Scottish fans invaded Newcastle. The home side scored twice which led to a pitch invasion by the away supporters. The two teams were taken off the field while the police restored order. The game was eventually finished and the 2-0 victory saw Newcastle go into the final.

Right: The front page of the *Daily Express,* the day after the Fairs Cup semi-final against Rangers. The top photograph shows a member of the St John Ambulance carrying an injured fan away from the trouble.

I looked up into the air and saw something glittering. Then I realised what it was. The light was catching hundred of bottles which had been thrown in the air. All of a sudden there were hundreds of empty Brown Ale bottles lying around. The bottles were then followed by hundreds of Rangers' supporters running on to the pitch.

George Hoare

When the bottles were thrown on to the pitch it was a bit like the film *Henry V* when all the arrows get fired into the air. The police marched on to the pitch, quelled the trouble and marched off again to rapturous applause from the Newcastle fans. The police were heroes to us because we didn't want the game to be called off – we were winning.

Bill Saunders

Rangers fans and police on the pitch during the semi-final at St James' Park.

A more peaceful scene on the pitch at St James' after Newcastle's return from the Fairs Cup final to show supporters the trophy they had won.

Newcastle's centre forward Wyn Davies charges towards goal while challenged by Sunderland's right back, Cecil Irwin. In goal is Jimmy Montgomery. Sunderland won this derby match, played on 29th October 1966, 3-0 with goals from George Herd, Neil Martin and George Mulhall. The last season of the decade saw the two rivals play their 100th derby. The game on 27th March 1970 was a 1-1 draw. After 100 matches the record between the two teams was 36 wins each and 28 draws.

Young Sunderland and Newcastle fans wait for the gates to open at Roker Park for the derby game on 30th December 1967.

Newcastle supporters show their colours outside Roker Park in December 1967. The game ended 3-3.

Derby Memories

I'm a Newcastle supporter and I remember going to derby matches in the 1960s. I would stand shoulder to shoulder with Sunderland fans and thoroughly enjoyed myself. There was a little bit of good humoured banter, a little leg pulling, but nothing nasty or malicious.

Bill Saunders

The rain was terrible on the day of the derby game at St James' Park in 1964. I was standing in the queue outside when someone walked past and said the game was off because the pitch was waterlogged. Everyone around us just walked away. When I got home I found out the game had been played and that it was just a rumour the match was off. My dad couldn't stop laughing when he found out what I had done.

Harry Clark

For one game against Sunderland in the 1960s I couldn't get into St James' Park because the ground was full. So I climbed up on to the roof of one of the houses overlooking the ground and watched the game from there. When I climbed down I was covered in soot from the chimneys. I was wearing a suit and it was absolutely filthy.

Ron Collins

Above: Goalkeeper Lev Yashin of the USSR keeps tight hold of the ball during the World Cup quarter-final tie against Hungary at Sunderland's Roker Park on 23rd July 1966. The USSR won 2-1 but were beaten by West Germany in the semi-final played at Goodison Park.

Sunderland's ground also hosted games during the group stage of the competition. Another venue used during the World Cup was Ayresome Park in Middlesbrough which witnessed one of the biggest upsets in football history when North Korea beat Italy 1-0.

England faced Uruguay, Mexico, France, Argentina and Portugal on their way to the memorable final at Wembley on 30th July 1966. West Germany were beaten 4-2 in extra-time with a Geoff Hurst hat-trick and a goal from Martin Peters.

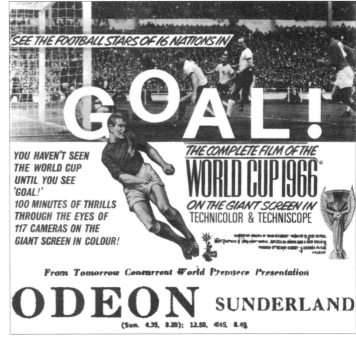

Above: An advert for the 1966 World Cup film, *Goal!*, being shown at the Odeon in Sunderland. In the days before colour television, it was the chance to relive England's victory in 'technicolor'.

Left: Two of England's World Cup winners, Bobby and Jack Charlton are given a heroes' welcome on a visit to their home town of Ashington. Bobby scored twice in the semi-final win over Portugal as well as getting a memorable goal in the group stage against Mexico.

Movie Memories

Some of the most popular movies in Britain in the early 1960s were the so called 'kitchen sink' films such as *Saturday Night and Sunday Morning, A Taste of Honey, The Loneliness of the Long Distance Runner, This Sporting Life* and *A Kind of Loving.* They portrayed a more realistic look at life than had been seen in cinema previously, with working class characters, adult themes and location filming, often in the North of England. Most of the films were adapted from plays or novels by writers including Alan Sillitoe, Shelagh Delaney and Stan Barstow while introducing actors like Albert Finney, Tom Courtenay, Alan Bates and Rita Tushingham.

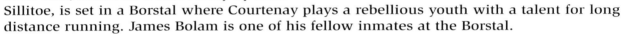

Sunderland-born actor James Bolam appeared in two of these classic dramas. *Right*: Bolam alongside Tom Courtenay in *The Loneliness of the Long Distance Runner.* The 1962 film, based on a short story by Alan Sillitoe, is set in a Borstal where Courtenay plays a rebellious youth with a talent for long distance running. James Bolam is one of his fellow inmates at the Borstal.

The Sunderland actor was also in *A Kind of Loving* which was very popular at the British box office in 1962. Adapted from a Stan Barstow novel, the film tells the story of a young Lancashire couple – played by Alan Bates and June Ritchie. Bolam is a friend of the Alan Bates character and in one memorable scene they go to watch a Bolton Wanderers football match. They are seen on the left, standing on the terraces of Burnden Park.

The success of the kitchen sink films led to more filming on location outside of London and in 1961 Tyneside was seen on the big screen in the crime drama *Payroll.* Michael Craig (*left*) leads a gang who rob a payroll van with scenes filmed in Newcastle City Centre and Quayside, Gateshead, Tynemouth and Lemington.

Below: The poster for *Payroll* featuring actors Michael Craig, Francoise Prevost, Billie Whitelaw, William Lucas and Tom Bell.

A number of other films were made in the North East during the 1960s: *Becket* (Alnwick and Bamburgh), *Cul-de-Sac* (Holy Island) and *Women in Love* (Gateshead, North Shields and Bedlington).

Right: Patrick McGoohan and Janet Munro in a scene from *Life For Ruth* which was filmed in Seaham. The 1962 film was directed by Basil Dearden whose productions often featured subjects that were seen as controversial in the 1950s and '60s. These films included *The Blue Lamp* (the murder of a policeman), *The Gentle Gunman* (IRA), *Violent Playground* (juvenile delinquents) and *Sapphire* (race relations).

Life For Ruth was the story of a father, played by Michael Craig, who because of his religious beliefs refuses to allow his daughter, Ruth, to have a life-saving blood transfusion. Janet Munro was Ruth's mother while McGoohan played a doctor. Eight-year-old Lynn Taylor from Cullercoats was Ruth. Basil Dearden often used locations outside of London and he chose Seaham and its dramatic North Sea coastline as the ideal setting for this intense drama.

Joe Robinson (*left*) was born in Newcastle in 1927 and first found fame as a wrestler. He won the European Heavyweight title in 1952 before an injury ended his career. Joe turned to acting and made his film debut in *A Kid For Two Farthings* in 1955. Further roles in the 1960s included appearances in: *The Two Faces of Dr Jekyll, Carry on Regardless, Barabbas, The Loneliness of the Long Distance Runner* and *Doctor in Distress*. The actor made a number of films in Italy including the title role in *Thor and the Amazon Women*. On television, Joe appeared in *Hancock's Half Hour, The Avengers* and *The Saint*. His final film appearance was in the James Bond movie *Diamonds Are Forever* in 1971. He played a diamond smuggler who has a brutal fight with Sean Connery in a lift. After retiring from acting, Joe moved to Brighton and opened a martial arts centre. He died in 2017, at the age of 90.

Joe Robinson played a gladiator in the 1962 Biblical epic *Barabbas* (*advertised right*). Anthony Quinn is the title character, a thief who was sentenced to death at the same time as Jesus Christ. However, he is pardoned while Jesus is crucified. The film follows Barabbas' life for the next twenty years including when he becomes a gladiator. Joe Robinson is one of his trainers and takes part in contests in the arena in Rome.

When *Barabbas* was shown at The Queen's Hall in Newcastle, the price for the circle was 8 shillings 6d and 6 shillings 6d. Seats in the stalls were 6 shillings 6d to 4 shillings. At the bottom of the advert is a tear off slip for movie goers to book a seat. The Queen's was known for showing the big budget films of the 1960s.

Left: A technician feeds the special 70 millimetre film of *Barabbas* into a projector at the Queen's Hall. Most movies are projected using 35 millimetre film but epics such as *Barabbas* had double width film as they were presented in widescreen Technirama.

A poster for the film *Summer Holiday* starring Cliff Richard and featuring The Shadows. The musical, with Cliff and his friends driving their converted red, double decker bus around Europe, was a big hit at the box office in 1963. The Shadows also appeared with Cliff Richard in *The Young Ones* (1961), *Wonderful Life* (1964), *Finders Keepers* (1966) and had a cameo in *Thunderbirds Are Go!* (1966).

Left: The *Thunderbirds Are Go!* EP with the puppet versions of The Shadows on the cover. The group played three instrumentals and the song *Shooting Star* with Cliff Richard.

Virginia McKenna and Bill Travers in the 1966 film *Born Free*. Based on a true story, the actors played Joy and George Adamson who raised Elsa, a lion cub, and then released her back into the wild. Bill Travers, born in Sunderland, is perhaps best known for the title role of a Scottish athlete in the film *Geordie*. He married Virginia McKenna in 1957 and they made several films together. After their experiences of working on *Born Free* they became involved in animal conservation.

British films of the 1960s

Below are some of the popular and award-winning British films.

1960 – Doctor in Love
(top box office film in the UK that year)
The Angry Silence
Saturday Night and Sunday Morning

1961 – The Day the Earth Caught Fire
The Guns of Navarone
(the second biggest box office film in the world that year)
A Taste of Honey

1962 – Dr No
(the first James Bond film)
Lawrence of Arabia
(Oscar for best film)
The Loneliness of the Long Distance Runner

1963 – Summer Holiday
This Sporting Life
Tom Jones
(Oscar for best film)

1964 – Goldfinger
A Hard Day's Night
Zulu

1965 – Dr Who and the Daleks
The Ipcress File
The Spy Who Came in From the Cold

1966 – Alfie
Born Free
A Man for All Seasons
(Oscar for best film)

1967 – Carry on Doctor
Quatermass and the Pit
(Hammer horror)
To Sir With Love

1968 – Chitty Chitty Bang Bang
Oliver
(Oscar for best film)
Yellow Submarine

1969 – Carry on Camping
(top box office film in the UK that year)
The Italian Job
Kes

Days to Remember

The 1960s was a great decade for music with bands such as The Beatles, Rolling Stones and The Animals enjoying worldwide success. There were also many local musicians who may not have reached the charts but are well remembered in the North East. Below one musician, Raymond Soulsby from Stanley, recalls his time in the group The Solitaires:

In 1959, when I was teenager, I was in a skiffle group with Terry Lewins, both of us playing guitar and singing. Later I went on to play the tea chest bass. This was a brush shank fixed to the back of a chest. The top of the brush shank would have a piece of thick cord tied to it with the other end of the cord fixed to the tea chest. This was used as a cheap version of a double bass. An old wash board (*left*) took the place of drums as no-one could afford a set of drums in those days. The wash board player would have thimbles on his fingers and would rub them over the corrugations and this would give a rhythm sound of its own.

   We met Jack Hair, who had a good knowledge of stage presentation and who was himself a good ballad singer, and the three of us went around doing local charity shows. Jack told me and Terry to move on and form what was becoming popular – a rock group. By chance, at that time, two other teenagers were looking to form a rock band, they were Ian Herron and George Wilkinson.

   The line up was Ian Herron (lead guitar), Terry Lewins (rhythm guitar), me (bass guitar) and George Wilkinson (drums). All four of us were from the Stanley area. We looked for a lead singer and met up with Lyle Edwards from Ebchester. This was the original Solitaires. Six months of rehearsals at the Hibernian Club at Stanley followed. This allowed us boys to keep up with the hits of the day as well as some of the old standards.

   The first bookings were for charity shows and one of the best at that time was a show that would bring regular bookings. This was 'Friends of the Hospital' organised by local barber, Hughey McPhail. Local clubs in the Stanley area would have the show on at regular intervals with all proceeds going to local hospitals.

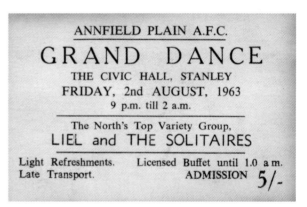

ANNFIELD PLAIN A.F.C.

GRAND DANCE
THE CIVIC HALL, STANLEY
FRIDAY, 2nd AUGUST, 1963
9 p.m. till 2 a.m.

The North's Top Variety Group,
LIEL and THE SOLITAIRES

Light Refreshments.   Licensed Buffet until 1.0 a.m.
Late Transport.   ADMISSION 5/-

Above: A ticket for a grand dance at the Civic Hall, Stanley in August 1963, where The Solitaires performed.

The Solitaires went on to play in clubs and dance halls all over the North East. We entered the 'Top Group of the North East Competition'. The final was at the City Hall in Newcastle and The Solitaires came third out of around seventy groups that entered. The competition was won by Sixteen Strings with Silver Dollars coming second.

   We later turned professional and played under the name The Geordies. We went on to play in London, Germany and Spain before breaking up in 1966.

The Solitaires, left to right: Ian Herron, Terry Lewins, Lyle Edwards, Raymond Soulsby and George Wilkinson.

Right: The triumphant North Shields football team proudly display the FA Amateur Cup to home supporters on their return to Tyneside.

Saturday, 12th April 1969 was the greatest day in the history of North Shields AFC when the club won the FA Amateur Cup at Wembley. Goals from Richie Hall and Brian Joicey gave the Northern League side a 2-1 victory over Sutton United. Sutton had beaten Whitley Bay in the semi-finals of the competition, denying North Tyneside what would have been a local derby in the final.

A crowd of over 47,000 at Wembley saw North Shields win their third trophy of the season. A unique treble was achieved when the team also won the Northern League and the Northern League Challenge Cup. One of the club's goal scorers in the final, Brian Joicey, went on to play in the Football League for Coventry, Sheffield Wednesday and Barnsley. North Shields' manager was Frank Brennan who twice won the FA Cup while playing for Newcastle in the 1950s.

Left: A unique photo of a game of 'pushball' at Houghton Feast in 1967. The referee blowing the whistle was the Chairman of Houghton Urban District Council, John Mawston.

Pushball was invented in America in the late 19th century and the aim is to push a giant ball past a line or between two posts. The first game in Britain was played at Crystal Palace in 1902.

Right: An advert for tenpin bowling that was introduced at Whitley Bay Ice Rink in 1966. Tenpin bowling was very popular in the 1960s and these new lanes were said to be the best in the North East. Features included: scores recorded on an illuminated screen above the bowling lane, the bowling balls returned within eight seconds and

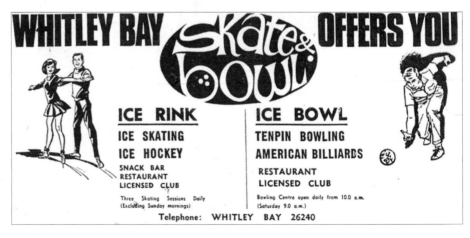

electric driers for hands to get a better grip on the ball. Another new attraction at Whitley Bay was American Billiards with the table cloth a gold colour instead of the normal green – said to be the first of its kind in the area.

Nights to Remember

Bewick's bar in the Five Bridges Hotel, Gateshead shortly after it was officially opened by Princess Margaret in May 1966. At this time the Five Bridges was one of most luxurious hotels in the North East and was the first 100 bed hotel to open on Tyneside in the 20th century. It was a popular destination for business executives, conference delegates and celebrities. The hotel ended its life as part of the Swallow Group and was closed in 2014.

Two photographs showing the modernised Earl Grey pub, Gosforth in 1965. The pub was advertised as offering: 'Good beer, a good home cooked meal and comfortable surroundings. You get them all.'

Left: A 1967/68 membership card, including a photograph, for the two La Strada Clubs. One was in Fawcett Street, Sunderland and the other was in Coronation Street, South Shields.

The La Strada

The La Strada club in South Shields first opened in December 1961. It had a Spanish theme downstairs, including a bull's head with a matador's cape and hat. The main upstairs room was like a German tavern with a boar's head on the wall. In the Monte Carlo room was a £400 roulette wheel that was brought from Paris. In 1963 the club employed forty-two staff and there were 3,500 members and another 2,000 on the waiting list.

Joyce Carlson

Joyce & Charles Carlson enjoying a drink in South Shields in 1962.

An illustration of the Royal Turks Head Hotel in Grey Street, Newcastle. In the early 1960s the hotel was serving some exotic food for that time: Chicken curry (6 shillings), Scampi Americaine (10 shillings 6d), Chilli Con Carne (5 shillings 6d), as well as the more traditional beef steak and kidney pie (6 shillings).

COME BIG STORE SHOPPING

As Gateshead's modernisation plans develop so too does Shephards ..... Gateshead's own major department store— the store that is ever looking to the future.

YOU'LL ENJOY SHOPPING AT SHEPHARDS
People travel to Shephards from all parts of Northumberland and Durham.   This super store has its own car park, over 40 departments on four spacious floors, a delightful restaurant, a snack bar, Escalators to all upper floors . . . and even a Barber's Shop! Everything for the home and family including fashions, furniture, footwear and accessories, fancy goods, linens, household appliances and carpets. The complete department store that's packed with exciting new ideas—*Come tomorrow!*

SHEPHARDS of GATESHEAD
WEST St. and ELLISON St., GATESHEAD.

Left: An advert from the 1960s for Shephard's department store in Gateshead. Emerson Shephard opened his first shop in the town in 1906 and he quickly expanded. By the Second World War he had a major premises in Ellison Street and eleven branches. A fire in 1946 destroyed the main store but it was rebuilt and opened in 1951 at a cost of £200,000.

In the 1960s there were a number of popular department stores around the North East such as Parrish's in Newcastle (see page 10) and Joplings in Sunderland (see page 16). Stores would often have their own money which customers bought and paid off weekly – a form of store credit.

Right: A 10d coin from Parrish's.

Right: Ernest Marples, Minister for Transport, cuts the first sod to mark the start of the building of the Tyne Tunnel at Jarrow in October 1961. Wearing a dark suit, suede shoes and using a mechanical shovel, the Minister performed the same ceremony on the Howdon side of the river.

Six years later, work on the tunnel was complete and it was officially opened by the Queen on 19th October 1967 (*right and below*). Vehicles started using the tunnel the following year and the toll for a car was 2 shillings 6d.

Right: When the Chieftain pub was opened in Cruddas Park, Newcastle in December 1969, a tank was invited from the nearby Vickers factory. Here Lt-Commander Barklie Lakin, managing director of the armaments division of Vickers (left) shakes hands with Henry Porter, chairman of Newcastle Breweries.

The brewery, on the pub's opening night, encouraged drinkers to: 'Try a glass tonight of Newcastle Exhibition, Newcastle IPA or Wm Younger's Tartan and you will find yourself, "making tracks" for the Chieftain again.'

Left: The interior of the Chieftain pub with tank tracks in the carpet. The pub had a 'tank' theme throughout. One counter had mounted on it a fibre glass reproduction of tank track wheels and track. Also in the pub was a small armoury of shells as well as camouflage webbing on the ceiling and behind the bar.

Right: *Esso Northumbria* on the River Tyne. After being launched from Swan Hunter's in 1969, the supertanker was to have a short working life and ended its service in 1982. Her sister ship *Esso Hibernia*, launched from Swan's in 1970, survived until 1983. Both vessels were broken up in Taiwan.

Leaving The Tyne

I can remember when the *Esso Northumbria* was launched – it was two hundred and fifty thousand tons. I was standing at Cullercoats when it left the Tyne and was so impressed by its size – it absolutely dwarfed the North Pier. Even though I had seen it being built in the yard and saw how it dwarfed all the buildings around it – I was still impressed.

Leslie Took

1960s Time Line

1960

March 15th – Manchester City sign 20-year-old forward Denis Law for a British record fee of £55,000 from Huddersfield Town.

May 6th – Princess Margaret marries Antony Armstrong-Jones at Westminster Abbey in the first televised Royal wedding.

August 22nd – The first performance of the satirical revue *Beyond the Fringe* in Edinburgh. It was written and performed by Peter Cook, Dudley Moore, Alan Bennett and Jonathan Miller. The show goes on to play London's West End and Broadway in New York.

September 15th – The first traffic wardens are deployed in London.

October 27th – The film *Saturday Night and Sunday Morning* is released.

December 9th – The first episode of *Coronation Street* is broadcast on ITV.

December 31st – The last man is called up for National Service as conscription ends.

1961

January 1st – The farthing coin ceases to be legal tender.

March 13th – Black and white £5 notes cease to be legal tender.

May 1st – Betting shops become legal in Britain.

August 13th – The East German army closes the border between East and West Berlin. Construction of the Berlin Wall begins.

September 16th – Two people die and thirty-five are injured when a barrier collapses during a Glasgow Rangers football match at Ibrox Park.

September 19th – The first Mothercare store opens in Kingston, Surrey.

October 25th – The first edition of the satirical magazine *Private Eye* is published.

1962

March 12th – Accrington Stanley, of the Fourth Division, resign from the Football League due to huge debts.

June 9th – A procession along Scotswood Road, Newcastle (*right*) is held to celebrate the centenary of the Blaydon Races.

July 20th – The world's first regular passenger hovercraft service is introduced between Rhyl in North Wales and Wallasey.

September 20th – The Ford Motor Company launches the Cortina, a family saloon costing £573.

September 21st – ITV broadcast the first edition of the quiz programme *University Challenge* with Bamber Gascoigne as quizmaster.

October 5th – *Dr No*, the first James Bond film, is premiered at the London Pavilion, with Sean Connery playing the lead role of 007.

October 16th to 28th – The Cuban Missile Crisis: The United States and the Soviet Union clash over the deployment of nuclear missiles in Cuba. An agreement is reached between President John F. Kennedy and Soviet leader Nikita Khrushchev and the weapons are withdrawn.

November 17th – The Seaham lifeboat *George Elmy* capsizes after going out to sea to aid the coble *Economy*. All five crew of the lifeboat and four of the five from the *Economy* are killed.

December 26th – Sunderland forward Brian Clough suffers a cruciate ligament injury in a game against Bury. The injury would finish his playing career. He goes on to become a successful manager with Derby County and Nottingham Forest.

1963

January to March – The UK experiences the worst winter since 1946/47.

A snowy scene near Burnopfield, County Durham during the harsh winter of 1963.

January 18th – The leader of the Labour Party, Hugh Gaitskell, dies suddenly aged 56.

January 23rd – The double agent Kim Philby defects to the Soviet Union.

January 29th – Charles de Gaulle, President of France, vetoes the UK's entry into the European Economic Community.

February 14th – The Labour Party elects Harold Wilson as its new leader.

March 27th – Chairman of British Railways, Dr Richard Beeching, issues a report calling for huge cuts to the UK's rail network.

April 6th – The Polaris Sales Agreement with the United States leads to the construction of nuclear submarine facilities at Faslane Naval Base in Scotland.

April 15th – Around 70,000 protesters arrive in London after marching from the Atomic Weapons Research Establishment at Aldermaston to demonstrate against nuclear weapons.

May 16th – The last serviceman is demobbed as National Service ends.

June 5th – The Profumo Affair: John Profumo, Secretary of State for War, admits to misleading Parliament and resigns over his affair with Christine Keeler.

August 8th – The Great Train Robbery takes place in Buckinghamshire.

September 6th – The Sindy fashion doll is introduced to the British public when it is shown in a television commercial.

November 22nd – American President John F. Kennedy is assassinated in Dallas.

1964

January 11th – The teen girls' magazine *Jackie* is published for the first time.

March 27th to 30th – Violence takes place between gangs of Mods and Rockers in Clacton-on-Sea, Essex.

April 20th – BBC 2, the UK's third television channel, was due to be launched but was disrupted by power cuts. On the same day, the BBC Television Service is renamed BBC 1.

May 16th to 18th – Mods and Rockers clash in Brighton.

August 13th – Peter Allen, at Walton Prison in Liverpool, and Gwynne Evans, at Strangeways Prison in Manchester, are the last executions to take place in the UK.

August 22nd – The first edition of *Match of the Day* is shown on BBC 2.

October 15th – The Labour Party defeats the Conservatives in the General Election. Harold Wilson becomes prime minister.

1965

January 24th – Sir Winston Churchill dies aged ninety at Chartwell, his Kent home.

January 30th – Thousands of people attend Winston Churchill's state funeral in London. He is buried at Bladon, near his family's ancestral home in Oxfordshire.

February 6th – Sir Stanley Matthews plays his final First Division game for Stoke City at the age of 50 years and 5 days.

March 8th – Two battalions of US Marines arrive in Vietnam. They are the first American combat troops to be deployed in the Vietnam War.

July 29th – The Beatles first film *Help!* is released.

August 6th – Peter Watkins' *The War Game*, a television drama showing the harrowing effects of nuclear war, is withdrawn from its planned transmission on BBC 1. It would be twenty years before it is eventually shown on television.

October 29th – Brian Clough is appointed manager of Hartlepools United.

December 22nd – A 70 mph speed limit is imposed on UK roads.

Throughout his career, Brian Clough was always happy to share his views on football.

1966

January 30th – The Action Man toy figure is launched.

March 31st – The Labour Party, led by Harold Wilson, wins the General Election with a majority of 96 seats.

May 6th – The Moors Murderers, Ian Brady and Myra Hindley, are sentenced to life imprisonment.

June 29th – Barclays Bank introduces the Barclaycard, the first British credit card.

World Cup Willie – the mascot for the competition held in England in 1966.

July 30th – England beat West Germany 4-2 to win the World Cup at Wembley.

September 15th – Britain's first Polaris submarine, HMS *Resolution*, is launched at Barrow-in-Furness.

October 21st – A coal spoil heap collapses in Aberfan, South Wales killing 144 people, including 116 children.

October 30th – A fire aboard the ship *The Toronto City*, which was being fitted out at Doxford's Pallion Quay in Sunderland, kills six shipyard workers and a marine engineer.

November 16th – The BBC broadcasts *Cathy Come Home* directed by Ken Loach. It causes a public outcry over the plight of the homelessness.

1967

January 4th – Donald Campbell is killed in a crash on Coniston Water in the Lake District while attempting to break his own water speed record.

January 7th to July 1st – *The Forsyte Saga* is first shown on BBC 2.

March 18th – The supertanker *Torrey Canyon* runs aground between Land's End and the Scilly Isles. At the time it is the world's worst oil spill.

March 28th to 30th – RAF and Fleet Air Arm planes bomb the *Torrey Canyon* and sink it.

May 25th – Celtic becomes the first British team to win the European Cup. The Glasgow side beat Inter Milan 2-1 in the final in Lisbon. Former Newcastle player, Ronnie Simpson, is in goal for Celtic.

July 1st – BBC 2 shows the Wimbledon Tennis Championship in colour. It is the first regular colour television broadcast in Britain.

September 20th – The RMS *Queen Elizabeth 2* (the QE2) is launched at Clydebank by the Queen.

September 30 – BBC Radio is restructured with Radio 1 and Radio 2 replacing the Light Programme. The Third Programme becomes Radio 3 and Radio 4 replaces the Home Service.

October 19th – The Queen opens the Tyne Tunnel (*right*).

1968

January 5th to August 21st – The Prague Spring:
The government in Czechoslovakia bring in reforms to allow more freedom for the people. The Soviet Union and its Warsaw Pact allies invade the country to stop the reforms.

April 23rd – The five pence coin and ten pence coin are introduced in the run-up to Decimalisation in 1971.

May 2nd to June 23rd – Civil unrest in France leads to strikes, street protests and the occupation of universities and factories.

July 17th – The Beatles animated film *Yellow Submarine* is released.

December 12th – The Durham Light Infantry is amalgamated with three other regiments and the colours of 1st battalion are laid up in a service in Durham Cathedral.

1969

March 2nd – The maiden flight of the supersonic airliner Concorde takes place.

March 4th – The Kray twins, Ronnie and Reggie, are found guilty of murder and are sentenced to life imprisonment.

May 29th – Newcastle beat Hungarian side Ujpesti Dozsa 3-0 at St James' Park in the first leg of the Inter-Cities Fairs Cup final.

June 11th – In the away leg of the Fairs Cup final Newcastle win 3-2 to lift the trophy.

July 1st – Charles Prince of Wales is invested with his title at Caernarfon Castle.

July 21st – Neil Armstrong is the first man to walk on the Moon.

August 1st – The pre-decimal halfpenny ceases to be legal tender.

The programme for the away leg of the 1969 Inter-Cities Fairs Cup final won by Newcastle United.

August 12th – Rioting breaks out in Northern Ireland. Later to be called the 'Battle of the Bogside', it is the first major confrontation of 'The Troubles'. Two days later British troops are deployed.

October 5th – *Monty Python's Flying Circus* is first shown on the BBC. South Shields-born Eric Idle (*right*) is one of the members of the comedy group.

October 14th – The new seven-sided 50p coin is introduced as a replacement for the 10 shilling note.

Also available from Summerhill Books

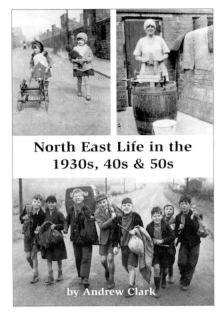
North East Life in the 1930s, 40s & 50s
by Andrew Clark

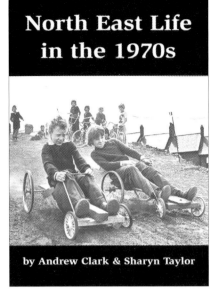
North East Life in the 1970s
by Andrew Clark & Sharyn Taylor

North East Life in the 1980s
by Andrew Clark & Sharyn Taylor

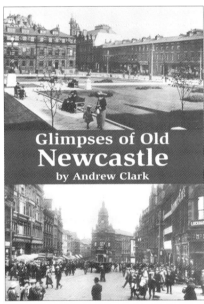
Glimpses of Old Newcastle
by Andrew Clark

Wallsend Best
A Personal Experience of the Rising Sun Colliery
by Ron Curran

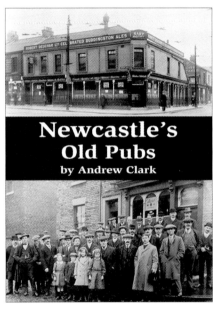
Newcastle's Old Pubs
by Andrew Clark

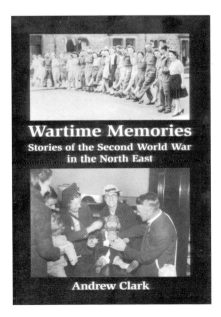
Wartime Memories
Stories of the Second World War in the North East
Andrew Clark

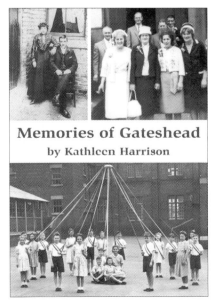
Memories of Gateshead
by Kathleen Harrison

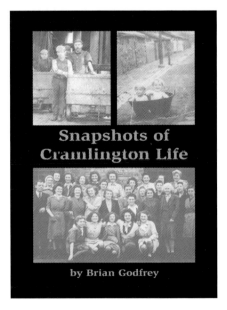
Snapshots of Cramlington Life
by Brian Godfrey

visit our website to view our full range of books
www.summerhillbooks.co.uk